PHILIPPE LEGENDRE

KIDS CAN DRAW

The Mountains

© 1993 Editions Fleurus, Paris.
Published by
Walter Foster Publishing, Inc.
23062 La Cadena Drive
Laguna Hills, CA 92653
ISBN 1-56010-274-8

Attention Parents and Teachers

All children can draw a circle, a square, or a triangle…which means that they can also learn to draw a snowman, brown bear, or woodchuck! The KIDS CAN DRAW learning method is easy and fun. Children will learn a technique and a vocabulary of shapes that will form the basis for all kinds of drawing.

Pictures are created by combining geometric shapes to form a mass of volumes and surfaces. From this stage, children can give character to their sketches with straight, curved, or broken lines.

With just a few strokes of the pencil, a mountain scene will appear—and with the addition of color, the picture will be real work of art!

The KIDS CAN DRAW method offers a real apprenticeship in technique and a first look at composition, proportion, shapes, and lines. The simplicity of this method ensures that the pleasure of drawing is always the most important factor.

About Philippe Legendre

French painter, engraver, and illustrator, Philippe Legendre also runs a school of art for children aged 6–14 years. Legendre frequently spends time in schools and has developed this method of learning so that all children can discover the artist within themselves.

Helpful Tips

1. Each picture is made up of simple geometric shapes, which are illustrated at the top of the left-hand page. This is called the **Vocabulary of Shapes.** Encourage children to practice drawing each shape before starting their pictures.

2. Suggest children use a pencil to do their sketches. This way, if they don't like a particular shape, they can just erase it and try again.

3. A dotted line indicates that the line should be erased. Have children draw the whole shape and then erase the dotted part of the line.

4. Once children finish their drawings, they can color them with crayons, colored pencils, or felt-tip markers. They may want to go over the lines with a black pencil or pen.

Now let's get started!

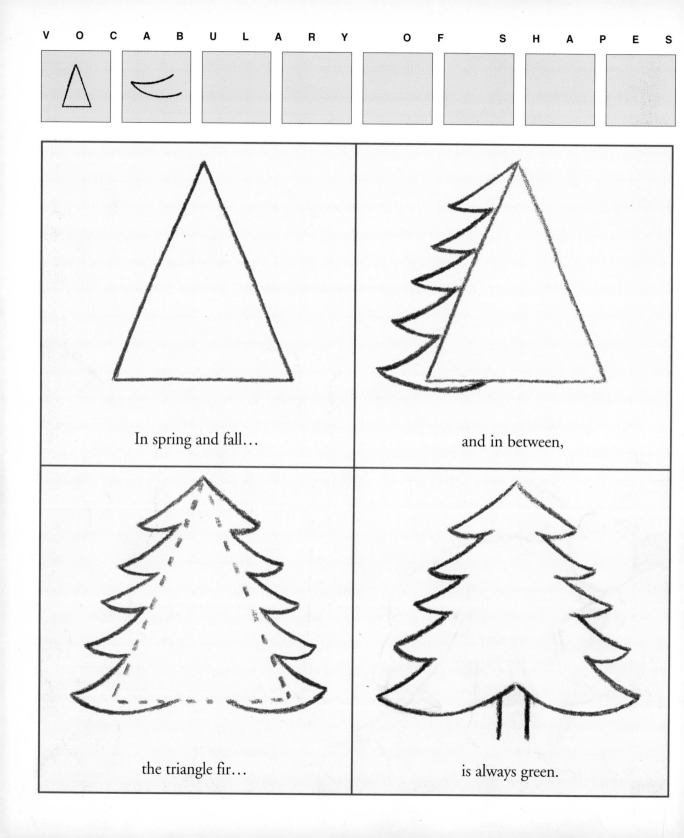

In spring and fall…

and in between,

the triangle fir…

is always green.

F_{ir} T_{ree}

With two circles…

the snowman is drawn.

When the sun comes out,

he'll soon be gone.

Snowman

With a round, hairy body…

and a nose that's square,

this giant animal is…

a cuddly brown bear.

Brown **B**ear

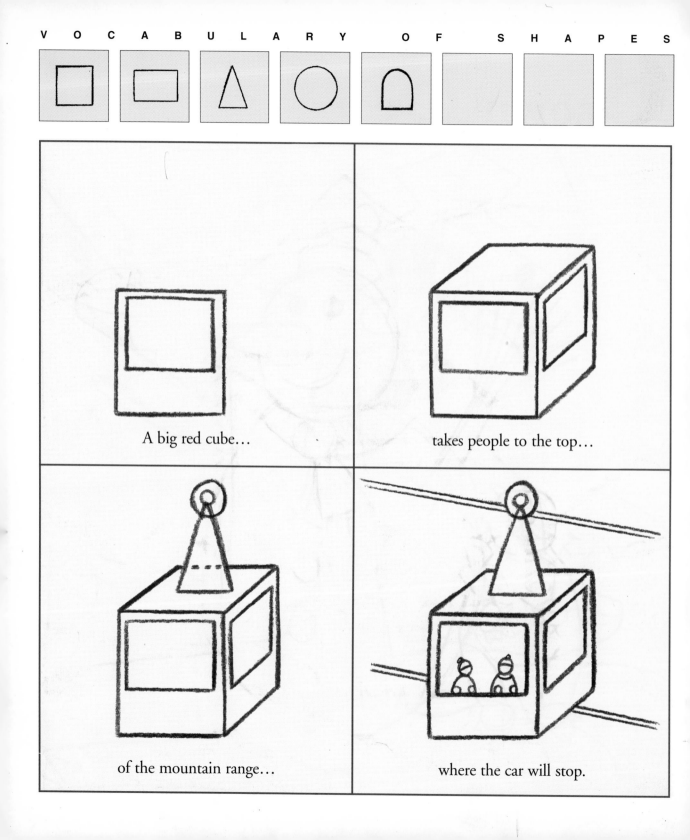

VOCABULARY OF SHAPES

A big red cube...

takes people to the top...

of the mountain range...

where the car will stop.

Cable Car

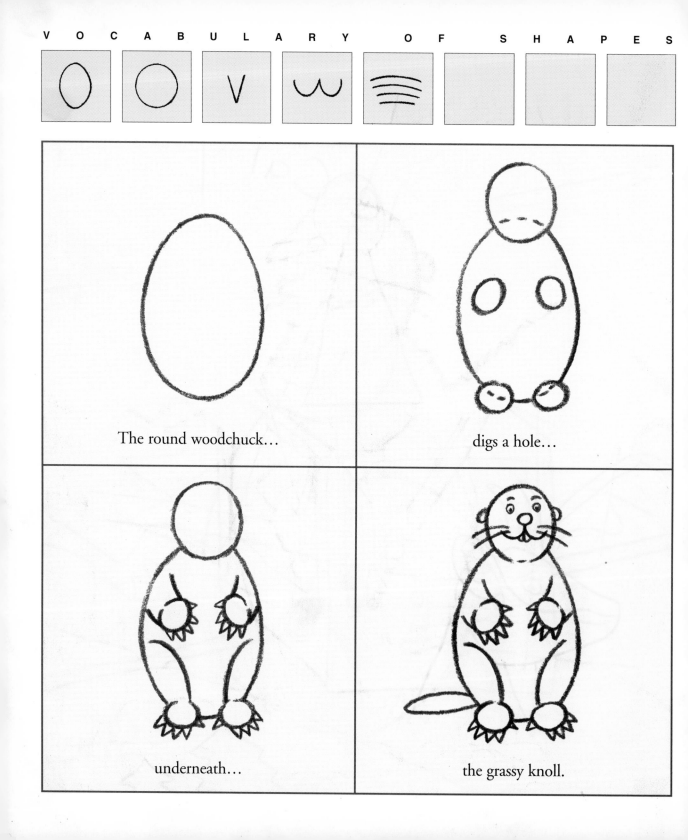

VOCABULARY OF SHAPES

The round woodchuck…

digs a hole…

underneath…

the grassy knoll.

Woodchuck

The antelope…

with rounded face…

climbs the peak…

with care and grace.

Antelope

To the square lodge…

the skiers race…

to warm their toes…

by the fireplace.

Ski Lodge

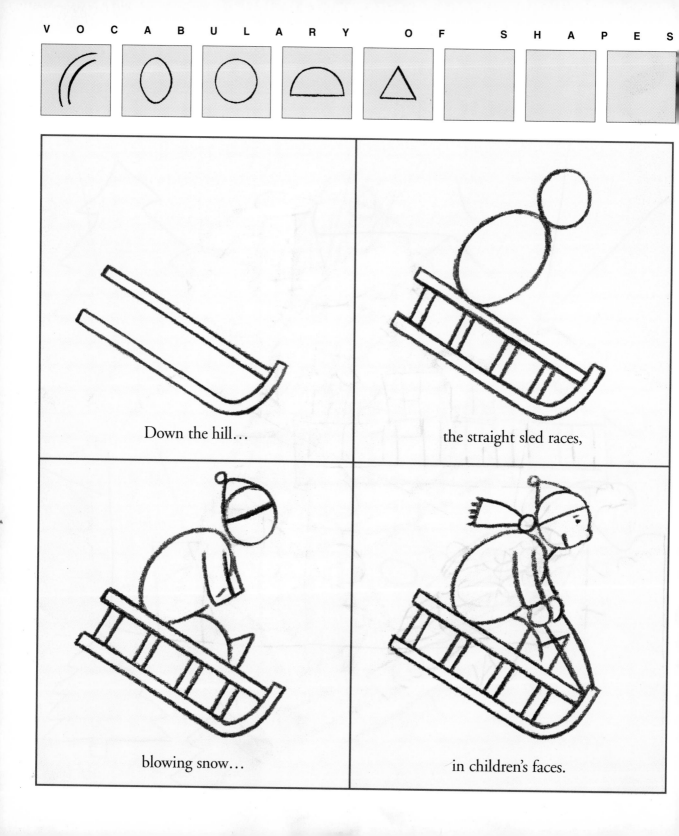

Down the hill…

the straight sled races,

blowing snow…

in children's faces.

Sled

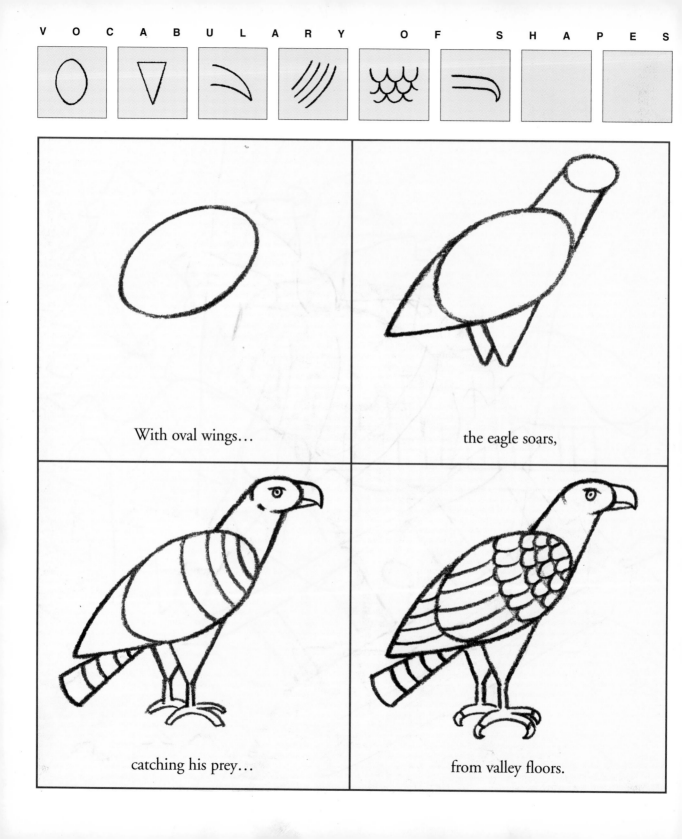

With oval wings…

the eagle soars,

catching his prey…

from valley floors.

Eagle

Blanketed in snowfall, it's winter in the scene.

But then springtime comes and all is green.

Draw-along fun for children!

With the "I Can Draw" Series, kids ages 6 and up will have hours of fun drawing amazing pictures of all the things they like best—animals, cartoons, creepy creatures, race cars, and more. Each book is full of colorful step-by-step illustrations with easy-to-follow instructions that explain how to draw almost anything by starting with the basic shapes kids already know, such as circles, squares, triangles, and ovals. Each 40-page book includes 8 pages of grid paper.

More step-by-step fun for young artists!

Our "I Can Draw" Drawing Kits come with an instruction book and all the materials kids need for drawing their favorite subjects. Each kit includes colored pencils, sharpener, eraser, and grid paper pad. These handy kits make great gifts for home, school, or travel.